Donated
in memory
of
Stanley G. Radhuber
by
his loving family

FLYING OVER GREENLAND

FLYING OVER GREENLAND

Poems by Stanley Radhuber

Drawings by Tom Hardy

PRESCOTT STREET PRESS PORTLAND, OREGON

Acknowledgments

Thanks are due to the following periodicals, in which certain of the poems in this book first appeared, sometimes in a slightly different version: *Buckbrush*, *The Chicago Review*, *Chiron*, *Concerning Poetry*, *Human Voice (Weid)*, *Local Earth*, *Lynx*, *The Mississippi Mud*, *Modern Poetry Studies*, *Northeast*, *The Northwest Review*, *Poetry Northwest*, *Poetry*Texas*, *Portland Review*, *Prism International*, and *The University of Portland Review*. Particular thanks are due *Poetry* for permission to reprint "Song in a Car."

ISBN (cloth) 0-915986-05-1
ISBN (paper) 0-915986-06-X
Library of Congress Catalog Card Number 77-83287
Second printing 1979

A Prescott First Book

Prescott Street Press
407 Postal Building
Portland, Oregon 97204

This project is supported by a grant from the National Endowment for the Arts in Washington, D.C., a Federal agency.

For Sharon and my mother and father

Contents

III

IV

I

Letter to My Father

Ours is a time of moving, father.
You found on the edge of this country
what teased the pack from Hungary
when the wheat rotted in their pockets.
Your bartered violin was the price
for dollars—the trade was gradual:
you played once a month,
then twice a year, once a year,
until the pain stopped altogether.

It was as though you were giving birth
to something, but in reverse,
taking in some great pressure, ingesting it,
stowing it behind the heart
like something contraband behind books.
I know that now, now that my hands
turn back like wrong gloves. Yet music
filled your days, and you wept to Schubert,
yellowing tears that mourn the ambiguities
that become gentle with the years.
In the family you were known as a practical man.

And in this time of moving, father,
as I cross fields far from home,
though not the instrument you wished,
I make slow music real enough
at times to startle an old professor
or young girl with braided hair
who leans upon her banister at noon.

The Road Back

We drove along the stream
through snow, found the pass
impassable, cars caught in a dream,
those crumbs cast upon snow
to feed a casual starling,
and turned our blind driving
back along the stream
black by then rutting the pure
fabric of mountain and sky.

Could we have said we were lost
and trying a last shivering match
to some gathered twigs
or peering for direction
over the round, cloudy face of a compass,
we might have had a story to tell
when we were elders docked in chairs
before fires lit by the young:
how creatures survive in circles
in the mindless drift of winter.

But we turned back,
took the road down without compass
in the dark of our sliding nest,
safe like some mute carollers
in the middle of a Christmas card;
down through somewhere where white meets night
going somewhere we couldn't see
at speeds we couldn't comprehend,
drugged by the oily blasts of heat,
staring off into the blank of direction.

Naming the Dark

South Dakota, near Kadoka, Badlands ahead,
broken points like teeth, a clicking jaw.
Danger taps behind the eyes.
The last lawn stayed in Minnesota.
We go the way we have to go,
above a crankcase sludged with oil,
beneath a mattress and only chair
lashed between the roof and stars.
Over the knocking valves
the prairie breathes,
humiliating our assault.
At last a neutral roof,
a shower in an old hotel,
drinks in plastic glasses that offend the light,
hot beef sandwiches, the juke box and sagging floor,
cowboys crouched like crumpled paper,
their eyes narrowed down to bone.
The black wind stalks the roof.
I stretch my easing body against my wife
and feel the hard land under her skin.
The night is a parabola of hydraulic sighs.
I cannot shut the neon out. I give the dark a name.

Toward Chicago

Somewhere near Omaha the great trucks
lined in rows in the mystical neon illumination
of the cafe night under the Citgo sign
wait, their throaty diesels knocking and rattling
while the drivers, all tattoos and easy whiskey,
linger in the loving country-western sounds
of a singer so nasal she's beautiful
in a cafe so hard with light
that it begins to look like marble.
All wear this place like beads;
and in the limits of function
there is a conversion to the beautiful,
as with the trucks, chafing, anxious,
until like weight lifters they are fully strained,
flanks hard, biceps enduring, pulse throbbing,
then passing us near Des Moines,
ecstatically musical and full of lights and sighs—
we are slow voyagers of the dark,
and how we love that rumble
and the flashing lights, the signalling of thanks
and bye-bye going mile by mile toward, ah, Chicago.

Flying over Greenland

I had hoped I wouldn't see it.
It was a place that served the mind
for whatever remoteness the mind needs.
Greenland! Like Conrad's Congo, or Madagascar,
it's off my map.

                    Or was.
Now it's down there breathing,
a surgical white room breathing
before the drawing of the knife,
full of negative life
like that village in the glass paperweight
where it snows when you turn the glass—

Eternity stops here.
That ice will cheat the worms and roots.

Look at it watching, turning like eyes in a painting,
slowed down to the square root of sleeping.

I don't need it. We're packed for Paris
and not yet frozen in flight.

I like it! Should I wake my wife?
I'd like to reach out, let some in.
We're insulated to everything
beyond these whiny engines,
even the dawn, salmon pink
and out there like a wall.

I'd like to let that in too.
But on this map we fly by longitude and latitude.
Dimensions only waver.

Leaving Chartres

The train ticks through the swaying landscape:
trees, vines, the usual cows,
hills gathering toward peaks,
the sky, O,
loveliest surprise of all,
a slowly revolving door.

A stillness in the land props up assurances
of bleeding stopped, wounds cauterized;
flesh ascends toward miracles:
grass greens, and
deep in furrows roots hold
Spring well anchored in.

Farther south the bees are out,
lovers open softer hours
as mindless pollen vectors
toward home,
and farther yet the sea
reaches locust and sand.

Sloped floor, stained glass, and spires;
may this symbol convert the heart:
the church at Chartres, spared such
human sighs
from love's negligence
or death's unswerving faith,

stands blessed of the Father, mortared
by hands that died. A way of grace
answers the prostrate flesh.
Mysteries
linger in the Lazarus dark
under the high rose window

that lighter than a penny shuts
the eye of day. Quietly as speed
Chartres fades, and fading
grows until
it penetrates all sky
above, all earth below.

The great world is in place, or seems,
and comforts even the dispossessed rocking
southward in a cinematic
train. The wind's
outside, flogging the back
of that farmer setting traps.

Inside, *les enfants* bolt and scream
past Paul Henried sneering in the aisle
all hat and insolence. The real world is just
a little frayed. Closer in
what's real won't surface til it hurts.

Under the Alps

You flow against this flesh
as though it were enough,
this flesh that every four or five days
groans and rocks
above you like bad weather.
  You are weary of travel and new landscapes.
  You flow against me as though I were enough.
Here in this square, this foreign place,
the bed sloped against the wall,
water running somewhere inside the building,
a breaking bottle, a cat,
  the silence of the square vibrating
  like the last far apart vibrations
  of a bass string
under the mountains sloped sharply
and humming like mourners carrying crosses
in processionals of wind.
  I am enough. I am everything.
I am old and my body is a mountain,
and my blood rushes
like high mountain water
curling down in donkey ears and lace,
only slower, more evenly, keeping time.
  I am enough. I am sufficient.
  I know the way to go.
I don't fall away when you lean against me,
needing me to fit your contours.
I know what you bring.
I welcome you for as long as you need me.
  And I take you against my chest
as though we were saying farewell,
and I absorb you
as the mountain absorbs rain.
I am not afraid.
I am not afraid.

Alpine Sketches

I sketch in the steep slopes of the Alps,
the houses, the cows, the child
with wild strawberries in his cheeks,
the woman reaching for wildflowers,
her feet measuring the slope of the mountain
as she bends,
and the man and his pipe by the blue car,
the clouds, the neutral light,
the tiny starpoints of flowers making slow revolutions,
the village huddled under gravity,
the tidy valley, the coiled river,
the stream and its surprising speed
and the ancient lamentation of the wind.
I sketch in the bullet-chipped buildings—
up here wars are over. I sketch in the end of wars
and the boy shepherding the cows
and the cow bells, and the sound of cow bells.
I sketch in the Christ of the cross,
the tears in his flesh, his mountain eyes;
and all the artists who walked here,
the English going south; the Italians north.
North; south; up and down, the circles,
I sketch in the circles that we make
around and around, ring beyond ring
becoming as large and empty as the sky.

Bringing Pears to Avignon

They assaulted our sleep, the lorries;
they came out of dream rumbling
like Napoleon's cannon
over the cobbled streets of Nova, all night,
all night bringing pears to Avignon.
We had flung open the balcony door
to the soft summer and the smell of time,
those Roman goings-on that floated in
from the old town where water trickled
out of pipes and along the street.

Caterpillars measured distance on the panes,
their brilliant humped bodies powdery as harps,
and the moon made Debussy miracles
in the thin sky of the deep glass,
while the dusty ochre walls of Nova
smoldered in the distant night lights of the cathedral.

So are we all novas, all doomed to dark.
We flare up,
make notes in the margins of our Michelins,
and burn away,
hissing out in a kind of mystical sibilance,
leaving behind only air rushing
into where we were, a final cosmic handclap
in the dark that erases our adventure:

Time takes us to the window and lets go.
What do we know?
What do we know?

Crossing

The prow leaps up, brings down the sky,
I clutch the rail, my fingers hurt,
and my heart beats into barriers of white.

What straits we have crossed, islands passed,
what mountains lifted out of green,
sights that heal these sores
like a Rembrandt come upon
on a Sunday afternoon.

And I have to tell myself
I am crossing the seas, crossing the seas,
with all this sinking blood
and the alcohol of this gull,
his eye, burned porthole in space,
so close, so close,
I feel its stare like a lance.

I take the pace of this deck,
walking in all my wounds,
measure this distance from stern to prow
in prayer, tears dried, no dreams, alive.

II

Crossing Worlds

Whose rain is this?
Whose highway?
Who owns the night?
One right turn and I'm gone
into the hills
into the dry under leaves
where legends sleep—

one moment of giving in
to the homing echoes
the madrigals of roots
   sonatas of snails
      the river bottom
homing me in toward,
toward places my blood knows,
marrow keeps secret—

one turn from this bare bulb
   by a nowhere gas tank
      on the highway
to a last breath perfect as rain
a love as large as the hills—
into the sheer weight of mountains
   the density of dark
where all breathing slows—

one turn,
            it's either now
or wait.

On the Origin of Sea Chanteys

All day his fingers moved around his nets,
mending holes with line held by a boy.
His body rocked to the feel of the sea
thick with fish. The river sang his tune.
Ask his dog, his wise ear twisted toward water.

Old man, I'm standing at your back,
and at my back the world is hunched.
It comes down three ranges inland,
then levels off to sand.
You turned just once to look at me,
just once.

The Windstorm

A freak windstorm gathered us
open-eyed behind the house.
It slid down from the trees,
splayed out leaves like cards,
old parchments that rocked
gently down in the slow, eerie light.
We took heart, for such visitations are rare,
and ran about with arms opened
as though we had been dropped pamphlets
that promised rescue.

And we ran far from our bitter house,
criss-crossing in the shape of prisms,
the shape of no shape like wound up toys,
cleansed of thought and passion,
clean as washed stones, as geese long necked
and pointed beyond latitudes,
as nearly physical as trains
that have just disappeared:

Refurbished, spent,
we hung on the slack strings of wind,
dancers gleaming like polished wood,
stopped.

Camping at Cape Lookout

We sit each on the other side of fire,
having beaten the fog to camp
among the cedars sloped from tips
bleached like some abandoned house
marvelously ruined in weeds and busted with the sun.
Night takes possession of the woods
whereupon the fire glows
and a buoy brings in ships.
The moon appears, then fades again,
and hunched like Bedouins
we toss our flaring matches toward the fire.
They leave arcs of smoke
and the sharp smell of sulphur.
In our sleeping bags we listen to things
drum on our tent top and roll . . .
and the distant wash of the surf,
that familiar, lonely sound,
and then the dark speaks,
and cloven hooves tick around the tent,
while cold nibbles us to our bones.
Nothing can be more real than this cold.
It chews away the warm lies of our lives,
sets its teeth into our marrow, and persists.
Sleep saves us, coming as it does like flowers
or stars found without looking up,
and planting us in galaxies of texture
like seeds in cotton, where we live until
skittish light breaks through the canvas at dawn.

Learning about Yodellers

Where I taught for seven years
the stairwell had a bad reputation.
It smelled of trapped flesh and salacious kisses.
Lovers leaned on one another
in the sanctity of their sexual abundance.
I turned my face, remembering
how much love hurt. Let them learn.

Gum spots were worn smooth and the color of mushrooms.
A tea bag spent a week lying on a landing.
Signs were everywhere.
The stairwell thrived.

One day a yodeller laid back
his deliriously blind eyes and opened his throat,
and sound warbled out like thrushes
and sprayed down the sharp inclines of the stream;
deer drank in the still palms of water.
Birds flapped softly in the greying trees.

He stood in the center of his sound
and turned the stairwell into a mountain;
his throat aching with the alchemy of joy,
his face stretched beyond known country
like footsteps taken up by snow:

It's all in knowing how to go,
unfolding wings, beating awkwardly for currents;
then sliding easily in a slip of wind.
A beacon tells you where,
if you just let go,
let go.

Learning about Pipers

The way the mountain falls off from its highest and wildest
into this park, cement walks laid out in squares,
mowed grass, a fountain, benches and swings,
you would think we'd gone far enough
toward imposing our patterns on the wilderness.
The wild side of you wants to go back up.
The side where the fear is goes toward the roof tops
on the other side of the park. There is always that.
One has to choose. Just about then the piper comes,
as he does nearly every noon in summer,
stepping off in slow, straight motion.
He turns sharply left and sharply left again,
putting squares within the squares of the park.
What is this ritual of making proud squares?
The sounds he makes are wild as Borneo,
full of white eyes and leaping thighs
coming at you from the other side of the wall.

Broncos

They are the best, neck against neck,
laced by an intelligence of blood and sinew,
muscles hard, animal nostrils pumped open,
gathered in flight, dark, shining, walnut and ebony,
in the yellow rodeo light

they circle in dumb insistence,
coming hard, all hooves and instinct,
their riders tossed off
into cones of darknesses
lying in the rickety arena
in the town in the valley.

And when they are broken,
tethered, their great curves dulled,
their manes quieted—
horses standing by railings, brushing flies—
or at work learning the rhythm of the shapeless herds
and the high strident whistle of cowboys,
their heads emptied from capture,
memory sleeping deep in the caves of their bones . . .

I walk out under the stands,
my heart beating for joy and shame,
through the beer cans and slop, into the rancid air
of this ten cents a beer town,
past the spurs of neon tavern signs
into the dark flopped down like leather,
thinking: resist, resist.

Back a ways the hills hump up in the night,
and further back I know there ought to be a canyon
and a river. The road takes you there and lets you go
beneath the sliding walls
where among the thistles and the tonguing snakes and lizards
you can ride the river home.

Making Love on the Afternoon of the Summer Solstice

by late afternoon a storm approached
a gift of cool air for your sleep
and unfitted from your flesh   I
was carried as though by water
along the bottom of a stream
to the pure beat of stone
one pulse that sighs
from the great
parabola's
thinnest extreme
one breath delicate
as wings   as precarious
as a drop of water hanging
from the eaves   but the heat held
our garden would grow through the night
the storm flew up another street   flesh
flowed back to me as though   alas   in a dream
I set my head to the heart buried in your ticking side

Song in a Car

Content behind radiator and hum of engine,
driving the hundred miles
through pastures pathed between stars,
I glide in the arms of her fragrance
singing decimated bars of Tristan,
Rudolpho, Alfredo, Hoffman—
deliver in strident passions the fragments
of my repertoire. Moved to song
yet out of song, I reach mechanically
for the radio, and static gathers
into low sound from the arc
of night beyond the swollen stars.
New Orleans . . . radio . . . act two
Tosca. Tubes crackle with the strain.
On local stations they rock and scream,
a woman scourges civil rights,
a man advocates nuclear war—
my mood broken, fragrance burned away,
I search angrily for the faltering act,
Mario tortured, Scarpia hot on Tosca
like a scorpion at a foot,
Tosca singing *Vissi d'arte*
then stabbing a man in ceremony
between candles—it comes in waves
like applause from overseas, spits
out in the tinny declamation
of my two-bit radio. Enough!
Nervous and songless I weight the pedal
and take a shrill B flat over the castle wall.

First Lament

Inside, the cry struggles to escape.
The day has filled your soul with gloom
and you remember the fog that charged over the bay
sending boats back with less catch,
and when the boat bucked up
   on the back of a wave
      you knew the first terror
of water. And the little things:
hopscotch markings on a sidewalk,
   full of possibilities,
                              hieroglyphics
if you could let the mind leap into their secrets—
and the sounds of thrushes
from the tips of trees, falling
down the ramp of sky like a knife blade.
Spring.
          Spring in this city in which you wander
and the trees in which you wander
remembering the boat on the bay
and the cries of the seagulls
wheeling around your head like white flowers,
and the fog drumming in over the bar
like things falling from trees.
Then the elevators and coffee
and you search for shape, for form
before everything presses into the uncertain, stunned mind
hanging like a yellowing light bulb
   surrounded by dark,
where you sat
                    after having absorbed everything
                    and being full of infinite possibilities—
you find yourself empty and murmuring.
You begin to formulate a cry,
and desire, that call in the fog,
slides through you like a cruel flower petal.

Your cry is deep in the earth,
yet you do not feel at one with the earth.
Only your cry is deep in the earth,
a root in the dark,
                    shut off and crying,
and your mouth is full of darkness
under the dew which distills morning—
your mouth is full of darkness,
your mouth
with pearls hanging from the corners,
tortured into shape, shaped for words,
your mouth full of darkness,
shaped for words.

Père-Lachaise Cemetery
(After P. Bourget and Claude Debussy)

It is evening, in Paris.
September. The fine scent of urine
that in August makes its way up from the river
like a thought emerging from the banks of the mind
still lingers, here in the cemetery,

mingles with the rich air of decay,
   the rotting flowers,
      limp stems hanging out of carts,
piles of broken flower pots—
   flotsam in this sea of gravel—
the dead smell of empty water pipes . . .

Here they lie, under stone,
these famous writers and their prophecies
remembered by the literate
who bring them flowers
then ponder the deep silence buried there.

The unknown are soon forgotten.
One generation tends their graves,
the next its own affairs,

but known or unknown all settle into the soil
under the city,
                    that dead dampness
undisturbed by plow
                    or the crack of sprouting seeds
or the cats crouched everywhere
flagging tails for war or love
or the lovers making love on a dare.

The dreary ship sails by.
Shades brush our faces in the evening air.
This is not a peaceful place,
not, at least, on this troubled side of death

among the monuments leaning
   like sails exhausted
with wind
               and slowly sinking.

You drop my hand.
You are anxious to leave these gates.
The city awaits, full of charm.
Be happy. Be happy, it says,

there are the chimneys and tiles of Paris
   shimmering in the last light
      above the shadowy streets,
the suede boots along the boulevard,
the ladies at cafe tables,
   their heads tilted as though in a Seurat.

Ah, *beau soir*, I come,
I come to drink the long evening in.

Lift the Heart

Lift the heart into the circle
of the hawk. He flies because
he cannot walk.

Lift the heart into the cycle
of the tree. It breathes because
it cannot see.

Lift the heart into the spiral
of the Angels. They dream because
they cannot tell.

Lift the heart onto the sickle
of despair. I love because
she touched me here, and there.

The Artist in His Chair

And what if the search suddenly ends this way,
in the soft chair by the two-hundred year old Chinese table
eddying serenely in a pool of green,
a glass of Genever by the jade plant,
Gieseking playing Debussy, and in your lap
that book about the Chartres cathedral—
and what in your head? Empty as the center of summer
after the seeds have given forth
and vines lie like clouds
draped over the horizon,
those clouds that drift like ideas?
And what in your heart?
What room there beside the fullness
of our great art?

Can I not continue on,
enter a world of nuances,
strained as the neck of a flutist
strains to send sweetness out with our despair,
fill the mind with oriental screens—
seek the luxury of reality
rather than the crude fact,

dream of being the month of March
with the heat of one seed sprouting
in my chilled breast?

Must I stalk that leaner landscape
of dry trees in dry air
where the hard cold holds in the hills

where in the blanched abandoned gardens
a jay wears blue winter on his breast
in the reality of the afternoon
and scolds the reality of the afternoon?

III

On a Path

This is the still heart of night.
I breathe heavily into a calm leaf,
lean my forehead into the stroke
of a branch soft as the belly of a cat,
closing distances the way a painting fades,
the way morning glory spindles into an open window;
closing toward the form of wind
stirring Japanese bamboo chimes,
toward the lift of houses on this hill
and the presentiments of shadows within shadows.
Up above the party waits with a yellow eye,
and I wonder what I shall tell them,
an incarnate lout, beery and full of propitiation
who has teetered near the precipice of form,
five legs from Adam and blessed.

Retarded Children

Pale and possessed they come forth
in their baseball caps and overcoats
in line zig-zagged like peels of fruit.
They scuff along hard on their heels, toes out.
Their eyes are burned holes in paper.
I think of God and the ceremonies
by which we fear what we are.
Then they run, released finally
from the secret insinuations of the dark,
the stillborn utterances of the blood,
and their arms paddle the air furiously,
and despite the hard axis of their animation
they dance toward form, close distances,
and the parts unregenerate and angry
catch each other in the dance until
they are giggling swans throwing balls
where no one can catch them,
then again arching balls
high into the parabola of blue
and running out
heads back and arms circled like the world—
six ballets, a slow explosion,
slow as the bead of water in the corn,
and their music is droning and ancient,
a priest-like sound, and I think of God
and how He must sit by the tree
and stare down at all the wounded,
waiting.

In the Orchard

Wonders of twilight draw a few to the orchard—
gathered by the still beach ball, under the apple tree,
the grandchildren gaze at the starpoints of fireflies
which have stopped their play. They point,
hurl cosmic questions at the grandmother,
who is watching darkness rather than light,
then leap and clutch handfuls of brilliant darkness
which seeps from their carefully uncurling hands.
Disappointed, they leap again into the jewelled evening,
chattering for her attention.
But she watches the cat, who disturbed
in the tall grass under the tree
climbs the short trunk,
slides along a darkening branch, and is gone.

Deer Hunter

Each Autumn he prepares his intrusion.
He fondles shells, hefts his gun,
sights in at cans, cats, his wife's back;
click! And his blood thrills,
arouses thoughts of slaughter.
He intrudes. Down wind from deer
the damp fern folds under his boots—
rubbed with oil while his family slept—
and he squints his eyes, cautiously
removes branches with his forearm.
He has stepped beyond his fear,
and once in so far must accept
his role. The crows caw, the fern springs back,
the wind brings him the woodsy mold
of ten centuries; the rattle of a woodpecker
startles him, yet despite his fear he craves
the knowledge of a dead deer,
the hot gun and the burned air;
and so he hunts, trembling like a deer,
head raised quickly from a brook,
nose in the air, soft eyes searching desperately,
his finger curled tenderly
around the moist steel of a trigger.
He hunts totally, like a clown
performing in circles before a wall,
always to fail, always to tremble
in the silence after a missed shot,
always to rack his gun with immense thanks,
never sure of what he did, or of why,
or of how to meet the winter,
white with sleeping animals, packed around his house.

The Swimming Hole

Stoical from motorcycle joy
they linger on the bridge over the swimming hole,
insect thin, blue jeans, nipples painted on,
all cock and sideburns; their girls
apple-gold under plummeting hair
dare them off the bridge
into the deep eye of the water.
I can feel their bird hearts beat
as they poise for diving.
They glance at the trees, suck air, and leap.
O, they float down unambiguous and infinite,
then disappear. With caught breath
we count the seconds. One head appears, then another
and another, water logged and full of panic.
They climb as in a dream up the surface of the cliff
toward the cheering girls. Then it's dare, dare, dare,
leap, leap, leap
until dark tends their pounding hearts.

Coastal Logging Town
"Hereabouts the signs are good" —Thomas Kinsella

Here, near the beginning of the horizon, nothing
is clear. The wind bodes cruel; creatures
hide till death turns up their lesions,
and strewn in rows along the beach they sing

that great music Plato heard westering
in the heavens. A dory takes the rock end of nature.
A few survive. Someone loses a conversation
with a saw and takes his beer by hook, telling
frantic tales by night.

And still men hunt
deer on the wood side of the highway, fish
for salmon in the sea. What shall they give up for Lent,
they who live hard on this edge? What excess
if laid aside might ease their predicament?
They live lean, between despair and wish.

Crabs

Dumbest of hard backed poorly perfected
abortively circular creatures, crabs
roll in like stones in the tide
that roars through the fingered bars
into the silent bay beneath our boats.
They tumble and knock and when the pressure eases
rig out their inadequate apparatus
and paddle at odd degrees—
who knows where they go,
these freaks of the seven seas,
what destination as salmon meet
up falls nature has arranged
for these inarticulate fellows
who drift in the direction of tides.
They change nothing, give no shape
to migration, will place with their clumsy claws
anything at all into their small mouths
that look like cracks in sidewalk.
They offer no subtle lore for catching,
but stroll Easter-like into any net,
still eating even as they are dumped
into bottoms of boats, where they heap
like a washed rose and blue festive rock.
Then we see their eyes far on stalks
like a Greek chorus, and listen
to the clicking and popping
of a language lost at the bottom of the sea,
a sound from the alphabet of stone
and diamonds, pools and fire,
the language of the world
before the fleshy creatures crept out
and turned to trap the sea with nets.

Sunflowers

Nine sunflowers against a wall,
heavy with the load of summer,
their stems thick but leaning
like telephone poles, their heads
over-large, once jammed with seeds like teeth.
Life ran up, now runs down, leaves
pock holes of missing seeds,
swelling at the rims, peeling
underneath. Summer was a fist.
Still, their obedient crippled heads search
for the sun, which is moving south.

The Country Couple

The dumbness of him
must wake in her a life
he can't caress
with his brute hands
nor hold in his fenced pasture
where the chewing cattle low
and nestle to his arm.
The woman quickened by birth
knows there must be more
and aches
before his stubborn eyes
to be nicked by life
in time, before that house
slides into the slope of field,
in time before
the absolutes of cattle, feed, and weather
close like shades her last eyes
on the last fumbling caress
of his hooved hands.

IV

The Woodchuck
(A diary of a hunt)

1.
He lives under the fallen grape arbor,
under the tangle of grass and old wood
which lies between the corn patch and the apple tree
behind a shack we once built to house some goats.
At six-thirty in the morning he eats
either the fallen apples under the apple tree
or the milk weed that grows
between the shack and the corn.
He may eat the corn.
In the evening
he will feed again.
As I write, the corn is about three feet high.
There are eleven rows of corn
with from twenty-five to thirty stalks per row,
a total of from 275 to 331 corn stalks,
say 300. At two ears of corn per stalk
the corn should yield at least 600 ears
(though many plants will carry three or more ears).
The woodchuck has already eaten two stalks.
Get the bastard, father said.

2.
In the tall grass bordering the collapsed arbor,
behind the shack, facing the apple tree
he rises on his hind legs and waits,
his back straight as a man's
pressed against a building.
When he thinks it safe, he waddles out—
he's fat—and sits in the grass under the tree.
He looks around while he chews
under the blue loft of sky.
He's mapped the landscape in his mind

so he can tell with one sweep
if something is out of place.
If something is, he'll pause, raise his head higher,
and stretch out the way a seal does
when he wants the ocean breeze on his neck.
But the woodchuck is afraid.
He might look you in the eye
and not be sure he sees you
if you are well hidden.
If he thinks he sees you
and looks into your eyes,
you shudder.
The sky is two moist, dark holes.
This is a moment of beauty and fear
in your conversation.
Then he'll run away.
He is always running away.

3.
Under the tree the grass is long and green,
the ground soft with tender apple leaves.
You can tell he's been there,
not by any natural signs,
but because there is much fear
under the tree and inside you,
and up the hill toward the house
where you hid and watched
and held the gun,
there is fear there, too.

4.
I held the gun.
I hate guns.

5.
Corn leaves are spaced alternately
on the opposite sides
of the stem, like semaphore signals.
Corn silks develop early
where the ear will eventually grow.
There is one silk for each potential seed
or kernel, never more kernels than silks—
count them, and notice how
the rows are arranged lengthwise,
always in even numbers
from eight to thirty-six rows.
Sometimes an extra feeding root grows out
about an inch above the ground
and bends down into the soft soil
like a finger bent at the knuckle.

When the silks are dry
the corn can be picked,
though it is hard to tell precisely
when the corn is ripe.
The silk under the husk remains green.
Good corn is indicated by thick stems.
Tassels grow on top of the corn stalks
and corn will ripen only when
the wind blows out the pollen
or when bees pollinate the corn,
when they take honey from the tassels
and pollen floats down
from tassel to silk,
male to female—
the tassel is the male,

the ear the female—
and bits of dried blossom
fall to the ground.
All this can happen
with just wind,
but when the bees pollinate
the tassels undulate in a sea of bees,
and the ground is white with shucks from the tassels.
Both the wind and the bees are gentle.

The woodchuck has now severed three stalks;
about six ears of corn lost.

A bead of water glistens after rain
in the tops of young corn stalks.

6.
The bees are in the corn.

7.
The pollen mixes slowly
with the silk. Roots feed all.
This is a most gentle copulation
between the roots and the tassel,
the bees and the tassel
or the wind and the tassel,
and then with the silk
and the earth and the sky;
and whoever eats of the corn
or who plants the corn,
three seeds in each hill,
is a lover of the earth.

For each of us in whatever way,
scattered into air
or lingering underground
in sealed boxes
only centuries can hammer open,
or quickly decayed
like an animal
head to tail exposed
to the elements,
are lovers beginning again
out of our own change,
as clouds to rain, air to lightning,
night to day, good temper to bad,
awake and then asleep.
There is no death
in this house.

8.
The corn is four feet high.
This morning
I lay in the tall grass
behind the house
and held the gun.
He was eating an apple
under the apple tree
when I fired. He looked up.
Before I could fire again
he waddled off into the tall grass
behind the shack.

I fired at him again
this evening

when he was eating milkweed
between the corn patch
and the shack.
He was enormous.
He is growing.
I missed him.

9.
Still only three plants cut down.
The corn is healthy,
the apples are full of worms but sweet
to the taste and smell from a distance
when their odor mixes with fresh wind
coming down the valley
behind the Palisades.
Under the tree, when the wind is still
the smell is pungent,
the heavy smell of change.

I sat under the tree, breathing,
and let my consciousness
drift in the smell.
My lungs are not strong enough.
God is rank.
It is difficult
to be holy,
but it is
the only necessity.

10.
His plan:
if you see the woodchuck
under the apple tree,

circle wide to the other side
of the shack.
Go near the corn patch,
then quietly
enter the shack
and tiptoe to the door
facing the orchard,
only fifteen yards from
the apple tree—careful of shovels and rakes
and the old plow laying up
like a ship in dry dock;
if you see the woodchuck
in the corn, circle the other way
from the house, go behind
the shack, past his hole under the ruined arbor
and behind the old asparagus bed
and the low branches
of a pine tree and slowly yielding dogwood.
If he is in the corn you'll get a shot.
If he is in the milkweed
in the near quarter of the garden,
the quarter unplanted this year,
he'll be closer.

I walked around to the left,
entered the shack
and by a window
raised the gun.
He was eating apples.
He was huge.
His eyes were brown,
the apples clear green,
almost alabaster.

There was no smell.
There was no sound.
He ran away.

11.
We hadn't seen the woodchuck for four days.
Then he came out at six o'clock
on a heavy, damp evening,
the sky all smudged down close
to the ground.
He was eating milkweed.
It was so quiet
I thought I could hear
his blood circulating
and his brain
sorting the confused images.
I shot at him from the house.
He flipped up
then scurried away
staying close to the ground,
his fat body
swelled up around his low head.
He looked soft and clean.
I thought of him that night
lying in his hole,
under the safety of the heavy dirt,
terror in his heart
as he watched the refraction
of fading light down the tunnel
and wondered about the hot sting
in his flesh
and when it would go away.

12.
There is no death, I thought,
but father said there is,
that it is real and black
and then suddenly unreal,
unutterable, a blackness of the soul
and no light, no light ever—
I could stand almost anything
but that.

13.
With only four stalks cut down
by the woodchuck,
and the corn coming in
so sweet we ate it raw,
I put up the gun,
while he, locked into his necessities,
pressed on with the hunt.

I prayed for the healing of the woodchuck,
that he may die in the way
of his kind, the way he knows,
in the jaws of a fox
or burst open by the sun,
and not by this metal sting
which is the creature who walks,
the way he reaches out to you.
That like the sap having run up
the trunk in the spring,
he may run down in the fall
until his thickening blood holds away
the world in a last dazzling

moment of bewilderment
before the great calm
and new ascension.

14.
He shot it,
tore the animal away from light,
then cut it apart,
the hind legs and forepaws,
severed the head with a kitchen knife,
busted the back,
pulled out the velvet stomach
and the singing parts that oozed
and squeaked like rubber through his hands,
and buried him in the garden
where already the stalks were browning
and drooping toward the earth.

15.
I carried his wound
and then gave it to the roots,
which will pull him out of the dark.

The Winter after the Assassinations

This is how we worship in the winter
under the dead weight of luminous snow,
around the card table, at the piano—
Requiescat in pace, while storms come off the sea,
my wife rolls me between her knees,
Requiescat, requiescat, this is how we pray.
  I saw three dawns
taut as the sound of Mahler tympani
and suddenly the mountains stung
like cold coins in my hand
when the sky lifted before snow came again.
This was the way the year ended.
  One morning we built a fire.
The children woke, and that was how we prayed,
our fingers around hot cocoa
on days off before the fire under the iron sky,
reading about the elephants
that stand in circles around their dead,
their hurt hearts calm, their peaceful eyes.

Waiting for My Daughter at the School Yard

Balls flying, shouts sailing into air
like balloons, red and green,
girls awkward as young birds,
ferociously at their hopscotch,
a boy lingering in a corner,
cigarette like aces in the cup of his hand,
and the fragile pistons of their legs
driving this way, that, or still
like cormorants in the slow wash of the sea;
the sudden flower of elbows, knees, heads,
a pristine, rootless, scuffling growth:
I pray you never trust beyond your play
nor let your hearts harden with fear.

Finally she comes—miracle enough—
coursing the school yard
like a kitten skating on a kitchen floor,
herself before her as she runs,
up and up upon her toes,
then she rises into air,
all her smile on my smile,
and into my arms.
They have to stand and look.

For My Son during the Cuban Crisis

I have fathered this crying man
who has no candle on his cake.
When I hold him in my arms
and caress his long shuddering sighs
and last tears against my shoulder,
his life is mine, mine is his;
no ceremony of slaughter at sea
shall stop my wishing.

I wish for my son soft breathing,
a place to lay his head at night
under trees and sleeping birds,
and for his own flying's sake,
I wish him parabolas of stars
and a landing of soft earth,
above all that he live in heart
and that that heart beat right.
And I wish he never know
this fear that he is sleeping through,
these days we catch our breath
and wonder where we made mistakes.

These things I wish my son,
whom I have paced asleep and rocked
before a lullaby of arms
and arguments in foreign tongues.

Catherine and the Animals

In her room the animals are arrayed in attitudes
unnatural in the plains and forests they stalked
for game. The burned out tiger drapes over a typewriter,
the bear props up a book. The elephant sags dumbly
in a corner, mortified by the slot in his back.
Hopelessly on his side, the giraffe lies twisted
in a cone of sawdust spilled from his broken neck.

They have been loved to death, then abandoned,
now for the turtle on the pillow who rules over
the spent snake, the sleeping lion, and the domestic sort
always kept behind the fence.
And always on the bookcase an egg with webbed feet
and little arms squats contentedly,
hatched out of the horrendous secret of an imagination.

At the zoo she cried. Their great hearts quelled in cages,
their storms paced away, the beasts roam only
the dead spots of their eyes. But how
their hearts must come to life when the wild moon
raises the streams, and everything that's awake
stares through the hostile light,
the air electric with fur, their blood
swelling as in the jungle under trees.
How the eyes must turn up, nostrils work.
She knew. She knew it all in an instant.
She said that night that the animals would be avenged.

When she re-arranged her animals
the elephant led a heterogeneous pack
ranked out like bowling pins, a phalanx
in which even the turtle had a spot,
and the pigs and cows, not knowing how or why,
fell into file behind the giraffe,

his neck braced straight with a safety pin.
It will come from surprising quarters, she said,
when the wind is still, the night as quiet as a table.
Don't worry. A few of us will be spared—
By that I mean, be given hearts like theirs.

Living in my own sadness,
I'd forgotten the animals by morning;
when she woke me with her wild, wild eyes and whispers,
she told me that something had started in her room.
She told me that at night she heard them breathing.

After the Dream

This morning the creatures are astir
routing out a meal at primes.
An opossum slides along the light
like a rubbing finger, a crow calls,
dawn slips coldly
over the still mansards of fear
like an ultimate thing with claws.
Caught dreaming by this chilled glass,
ear tuned for hearing, heart for belief,
I listen to my garden grow.
It cracks and roars, yields seed—a new grammar
beyond the pale meridian of fence—
At this moment all activity redeems
the heart and I feel a kinship
with the soft underneath of things,
the creatures and the sudden crocus
which blesses me, as I bless it—
Above is below and we are close.
Dark shapes the light, the world wakes
and we are where we have to go.

Stanley Radhuber was born in New York City in 1931. His family lived in Hell's Kitchen and then moved to Union City, New Jersey, where Radhuber was raised. His academic degrees include an undergraduate degree from Wagner College, an M.A. from Columbia University and a Ph.D. from the University of Michigan, all in English. While at Michigan he won two Avery Hopwood writing awards. He was a journalist in the Marine Corps and has taught English and creative writing at the University of Oregon and Portland State University. With his wife and two children he has spent much time abroad, especially in France, where he lived for a short while in Dijon. At present he lives in Portland, Oregon, where he works as a freelance writer and serves as Arts and Entertainment editor for *Portland Today*.

Tom Hardy was born in Redmond, Oregon, in 1921. He spent his early years in Oregon and received a Bachelor of Science in General Art from the University of Oregon in 1942. During World War II he was an officer in the infantry and the Air Force. After the war he returned to Oregon, where he did some farming and logging while continuing his painting and sculpture. In 1952 he received an MFA from the University of Oregon and in 1965 an honorary degree, the Distinguished Service Award, from the same university. He has work in many of the leading museums and has had over 140 one man shows. He has taught at the University of British Columbia, University of California at Berkeley, the San Francisco Art Institute, Tulane University, Reed College and the University of Oregon. In 1976 the Contemporary Crafts Gallery in Portland, where his many sculptures are as well known as the local landmarks, staged an impressive retrospective of his work.

Prescott First Books are edited by Vi Gale. This book was designed and printed by John Laursen during September 1977 in a clothbound edition limited to 100 numbered and signed copies and a first softbound printing of 500 copies. The second printing of the softbound edition is 500 copies, September, 1979.